BEST-EVER
BARBECUES

Consultant Editor:
Valerie Ferguson

HERMES
HOUSE

Contents

Introduction

There is nothing like the smell of a barbecue for stimulating the appetite – and it's such a fun way to entertain. This book is packed with traditional favourites, as well as some innovative dishes. There are ideas for every course and every occasion.

Meat and poultry have always been barbecue classics and there are mouth-watering suggestions for steak, ribs, chops and sausages. Seafood makes quick-cooking kebabs, while fish may be cooked whole or as fillets or steaks. Vegetarians can choose from chargrilled vegetables, spicy tofu kebabs and even a tasty pizza. And if you have never eaten baked bananas or other barbecued desserts, prepare for a whole new experience.

The introduction offers guidance on choosing and igniting a barbecue. Safety tips will ensure that your barbecues are hazard-free, healthy and a real pleasure. Recipes for marinades and relishes supplement the many sauces and dips in the individual recipes, and hints and tips offer suggestions to make each barbecue a real feast.

With step-by-step recipes and illustrations, your barbecue is bound to be a success. The only thing this book cannot guarantee is the weather.

Choosing a Barbecue

There is a huge choice of ready-made barbecues on the market and it's important to choose one that suits your needs and the number of people you usually cook for.

Hibachi Barbecues:

These small cast-iron barbecues are inexpensive, easy to use and transportable. Lightweight versions are now made in steel or aluminium.

Brazier Barbecues:

These open barbecues are suitable for use on a patio or in the garden. Most have legs or wheels and it's a good idea to check that the height suits you. The grill area varies in size and the barbecue may be round or rectangular. It's useful to choose one that has a shelf attached to the side.

Permanent Barbecues:

These are a good idea if you often have barbecues at home and can be built simply and cheaply. They can be built with ordinary household bricks, but it's best to line the inside with firebricks, which will withstand the heat better. Use a metal shelf for the fuel and a grid at whatever height you choose. Packs containing all you need to build a barbecue are available.

Kettle-grill Barbecues:

These have a large, hinged lid which can be used as a windbreak; when closed, the lid lets you use the barbecue rather like an oven.

Gas Barbecues:

The main advantage of these is their convenience – the heat is instant and easily controllable.

Lighting the Fire

Follow these basic instructions for lighting the fire, unless you have self-igniting charcoal.

1 Spread a layer of foil over the base of the barbecue, to reflect the heat and make cleaning easier.

2 Spread a layer of fuel on the fire grate about 5 cm/2 in deep. Pile the fuel in a small pyramid in the centre. Push one or two firelighters into the centre or pour about 45 ml/3 tbsp liquid firelighter into the fuel and leave for 1 minute.

3 Light with a screw of paper or long match and burn for 15 minutes. Spread the coals and leave for 30–45 minutes, until the coals are covered with a film of grey ash, before cooking.

Types of Fuel

If you have a gas or electric barbecue, you will not need extra fuel, but most other barbecues use charcoal or wood.

Lumpwood Charcoal:

This is usually made from softwood, and comes in lumps of varying size. It is easier to ignite than briquettes, but tends to burn up faster.

Coconut-shell Charcoal:

This is not widely available, but makes a good fuel for small barbecues.

Charcoal Briquettes:

These burn for a long time with the minimum of smell and smoke. They can take time to ignite, however.

Woodchips or Herbs:

These are designed to be added to the fire to impart a pleasant aroma to the food. They can be soaked, to make them last longer. Scatter them straight on to the coals during cooking, or place them on a metal tray under the grill.

Wood:

Hardwoods such as oak, apple, olive and cherry are best for barbecues, as they burn slowly with a pleasant aroma.

Techniques

Marinating

Marinades add flavour and moisture and are also used to tenderize foods, especially meat. Oil is usually included in a savoury marinade, the amount governed by whether the food is lean or has a relatively high fat content. Arrange the food in a single layer, pour over the marinade and turn the food to coat it evenly.

Basic Barbecue Marinade

This can be used for meat or fish.

1 garlic clove, crushed
45 ml/3 tbsp sunflower or
    olive oil
45 ml/3 tbsp dry sherry
15 ml/1 tbsp Worcestershire sauce
15 ml/1 tbsp dark soy sauce
freshly ground black pepper

Herb Marinade

This is good for fish, meat or poultry.

120 ml/4 fl oz/½ cup dry
    white wine
60 ml/4 tbsp olive oil
15 ml/1 tbsp lemon juice
30 ml/2 tbsp finely chopped fresh herbs,
    such as parsley, thyme,
    chives or basil
freshly ground black pepper

Honey Citrus Marinade

This is good for fish or chicken.

finely grated rind and juice of
    ½ lime, ½ lemon and
    ½ small orange
45 ml/3 tbsp sunflower oil
30 ml/2 tbsp clear honey
15 ml/1 tbsp soy sauce
5 ml/1 tsp Dijon mustard
freshly ground black pepper

Quick Barbecue Relish

This relish is very easy and quick to prepare and will liven up barbecued sausages, burgers and steaks. It has a tangy flavour.

45 ml/3 tbsp sweet pickle
15 ml/1 tbsp Worcestershire sauce
30 ml/2 tbsp tomato ketchup
10 ml/2 tsp prepared mustard
15 ml/1 tbsp cider vinegar
30 ml/2 tbsp brown sauce

Cooking in Foil

Delicate foods, or foods that are best if they are cooked in their own juices, can be cooked in foil either on the grill rack or directly in the coals of the fire with more robust items, such as potatoes and squash.

1 Cut two pieces of heavy-duty foil, making a double layer large enough to wrap the food. Lightly grease the foil with melted butter or oil, then place the food in the centre of the foil and add any flavourings or seasonings.

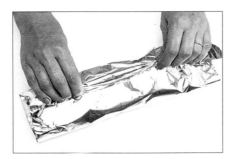

2 Wrap parcels securely, twisting the edges of the foil together, so that the juices cannot escape during cooking.

Safety Tips: Barbecueing is a perfectly safe method of cooking if it's done sensibly – use these simple guidelines as a basic checklist.
• Make sure the barbecue is sited on a firm surface and is stable and level before lighting. Once lit, do not move it.
• Keep the barbecue sheltered from wind, away from trees and shrubs.
• Always follow the manufacturer's instructions for your barbecue.
• Don't try to hasten the fire and never pour flammable liquid on to it.
• Keep children (and pets) away from the fire and always make sure the cooking is supervised by adults.
• Keep perishable foods cold until you're ready to cook.
• Make sure meat such as burgers, sausages and poultry are thoroughly cooked – there should be no trace of pink in the juices.
• Wash your hands after handling raw meats and before touching other foods; don't use the same utensils for raw and cooked foods.
• Have a bucket of sand and a water spray on hand.
• Trim excess fat from meat and don't make marinades too oily; fat can cause dangerous flare-ups.
• Use long-handled barbecue tools for turning and basting; keep long oven gloves handy.
• Keep raw foods away from cooked foods, to prevent possible cross-contamination.

Charred Artichokes with Lemon Oil Dip

Roasting over a barbecue is a wonderful way to cook young artichokes.
Finish off the dip while the artichokes are cooling slightly.

Serves 4

INGREDIENTS
15 ml/1 tbsp lemon juice or white
    wine vinegar
2 globe artichokes, trimmed
1 lemon
12 garlic cloves, unpeeled
90 ml/6 tbsp olive oil
sea salt
sprigs of flat leaf parsley,
    to garnish

2 Using a sharp knife thinly pare two strips of lemon rind. Scrape away any pith. Place the rind in a small pan with water to cover. Bring to the boil, then simmer for 5 minutes. Drain, refresh in cold water, then chop roughly. Set it aside. Squeeze the juice and set aside.

1 Add the lemon juice or vinegar to a bowl of cold water. Cut each artichoke lengthways into wedges. Pull the hairy choke out from the centre of each wedge, then drop them into the acidulated water.

3 Drain the artichoke wedges and place in a foil tray or roasting tin with the garlic. Add half the oil and toss to coat. Sprinkle with salt and barbecue for 15–20 minutes, turning once or twice, until tender and a little charred.

4 Arrange the cooked artichokes on a serving plate and set aside to cool for about 5 minutes. Using the back of a fork, gently flatten the garlic cloves so that the flesh squeezes out of the skins.

5 Transfer the garlic flesh to a bowl, mash to a purée, then add the lemon rind. Using the fork, whisk the remaining olive oil and the lemon juice into the garlic mixture. Serve the artichokes warm with the lemon dip.

Spicy Chicken Wings

These deliciously sticky bites will appeal to adults and children alike, although younger eaters might prefer a little less chilli.

Serves 4

INGREDIENTS
8 plump chicken wings
2 large garlic cloves, cut into slivers
15 ml/1 tbsp olive oil
15 ml/1 tbsp paprika
5 ml/1 tsp chilli powder
5 ml/1 tsp dried oregano
5 ml/1 tsp salt
5 ml/1 tsp freshly ground black pepper
lime wedges, to serve

1 Using a small sharp knife, make one or two cuts in the skin of each chicken wing and carefully slide a sliver of garlic under the skin. Brush the wings with the olive oil.

2 In a large bowl, stir together the paprika, chilli powder, oregano, salt and black pepper. Add the chicken wings and toss together until very lightly coated in the mixture.

3 Barbecue the chicken wings for 15 minutes, until they are cooked through with a blackened, crispy skin. Serve with lime wedges.

VARIATION: Chunks of chicken breast and small thighs may also be cooked in this way.

Barbecued Mini Ribs

Ribs are always a barbecue favourite. Here they are coated in a rich sauce with just a hint of spice.

Serves 6–8

INGREDIENTS
1 sheet of pork ribs,
    about 675 g/1½ lb
90 ml/6 tbsp sweet sherry
15 ml/1 tbsp tomato purée
5 ml/1 tsp soy sauce
2.5 ml/½ tsp Tabasco sauce
15 ml/1 tbsp light
    muscovado sugar
30 ml/2 tbsp seasoned flour
salt

1 Separate the ribs, then, using a heavy knife, cut each rib in half widthways to make about 30 pieces.

2 Mix together the sherry, tomato purée, soy sauce, Tabasco and sugar in a bowl. Stir in 2.5 ml/½ tsp salt.

3 Toss the ribs in the seasoned flour in a strong plastic bag, then dip each rib separately in the sherry sauce.

4 Arrange the ribs on the barbecue rack and cook over hot coals for 30–40 minutes, until cooked through and a little charred. Sprinkle with salt and serve at once.

VARIATION: Use freshly squeezed orange juice instead of sherry.

Koftas

A fun way to serve spicy minced lamb. These tasty kebabs are packed with flavours from the Mediterranean.

Serves 4

INGREDIENTS
300 ml/½ pint/1¼ cups Greek yogurt
¼ cucumber, diced
30 ml/2 tbsp fresh mint, finely chopped
salt and freshly ground black pepper
450 g/1 lb/4 cups minced lamb
75 g/3 oz/1½ cups fresh
    wholemeal breadcrumbs
1 onion, grated
5 ml/1 tsp ground cumin
2 garlic cloves, crushed
1 egg, beaten
60 ml/2 fl oz/¼ cup lamb or chicken stock
green salad, to serve

1 To make the yogurt dip beat the yogurt in a small bowl until smooth. Add the diced cucumber and mint and stir well. Season to taste with salt and freshly ground black pepper. Refrigerate until needed.

2 Place the minced lamb in a bowl and mash thoroughly with a fork to form a fairly smooth paste.

COOK'S TIP: Soak the wooden kebab skewers in cold water for 30 minutes before using to prevent them from burning.

3 Add the breadcrumbs and onion. Stir in the ground cumin and garlic. Season well to taste with salt and freshly ground black pepper.

4 Stir in the beaten egg and lamb or chicken stock with a fork. Using your hands, bind the mixture together until it is smooth.

5 Press the meat mixture into short, fat "sausage" shapes by rolling small quantities with lightly floured hands. Line up in rows.

6 Thread the "sausages" on to the prepared wooden kebab skewers (see Cook's Tip) and barbecue over medium coals for 30 minutes, turning occasionally. Serve the koftas with the yogurt, cucumber and mint dip and a crisp green salad.

Three-colour Fish Kebabs

Don't marinate the fish for more than an hour or the lemon juice will break down the fibres and it will be difficult not to overcook it.

Serves 4

INGREDIENTS
120 ml/4 fl oz/½ cup olive oil
finely grated rind and juice of
    1 large lemon
5 ml/1 tsp crushed chilli flakes
350 g/12 oz monkfish fillet, cubed
350 g/12 oz swordfish fillet, cubed
350 g/12 oz thick salmon fillet or
    steak, cubed
2 red, yellow or orange peppers, seeded and
    cut into squares
30 ml/2 tbsp finely chopped fresh
    flat leaf parsley
salt and freshly ground black pepper

FOR THE SWEET TOMATO &
CHILLI SALSA
225 g/8 oz ripe tomatoes,
    finely chopped
1 garlic clove, crushed
1 fresh red chilli, seeded
    and chopped
45 ml/3 tbsp extra virgin olive oil
15 ml/1 tbsp lemon juice
15 ml/1 tbsp finely chopped fresh
    flat leaf parsley
pinch of sugar

1 Put the oil in a shallow glass or china bowl and add the lemon rind and juice, the chilli flakes and pepper to taste. Whisk to combine, then add the fish chunks. Turn to coat evenly.

2 Add the pepper squares, stir, then cover and marinate in a cool place for 1 hour, turning occasionally.

3 Meanwhile, make the salsa by mixing all the ingredients in a bowl and seasoning to taste with salt and pepper. Cover and chill until required.

4 Thread the fish and peppers on to eight oiled metal skewers, reserving the marinade. Barbecue the skewered fish for 5–8 minutes, turning once. Heat the reserved marinade in a small pan at the side of the barbecue.

5 Stir the chopped flat leaf parsley into the heated marinade with salt and freshly ground black pepper to taste. Serve the fish kebabs hot, with the marinade spooned over the top, accompanied by the sweet tomato and chilli salsa.

VARIATION: Use fresh tuna instead of swordfish if you prefer. It has a similar meaty texture.

Salmon with Herb Marinade

Make the best use of summer herbs in this marinade, which is designed for the barbecue. Use any combination, depending on your personal taste and what you have to hand.

Serves 4

INGREDIENTS
4 salmon steaks
green salad, to serve

FOR THE MARINADE
fresh herb sprigs, such as chervil,
    thyme, parsley, sage, chives,
    rosemary, oregano
90 ml/6 tbsp olive oil
45 ml/3 tbsp tarragon vinegar
1 garlic clove, crushed
2 spring onions, chopped
salt and freshly ground
    black pepper

2 Mix the chopped herbs with the olive oil, tarragon vinegar, garlic and spring onions and season to taste with salt and freshly ground black pepper.

3 Place the fish steaks in a bowl and pour over the prepared herb marinade. Cover with clear film and leave in a cool place for 4–6 hours.

1 For the marinade, discard any coarse stalks or damaged leaves from the herbs, then chop very finely. You will need two tablespoons for the marinade. Any remaining chopped herbs could be sprinkled over the fish or salad.

VARIATION: This marinade would be equally successful with veal, chicken, pork, lamb or other kinds of firm-fleshed fish.

4 Brush the pieces of fish with the marinade and cook on the barbecue, turning occasionally, for 5–8 minutes, until they are tender. Brush with the marinade while they cook. Serve with a green salad.

Barbecued Trout

The pretty pink flesh and strong flavour of rainbow trout encourages a very simple approach, like this one, when it comes to cooking it.

Serves 4

INGREDIENTS
50 g/2 oz/4 tbsp butter, melted
10 ml/2 tsp chopped fresh dill
10 ml/2 tsp chopped fresh flat
   leaf parsley
4 trout fillets
45–60 ml/3–4 tbsp lemon juice
salt and freshly ground
   black pepper
baby red Swiss chard leaves
   and flat leaf parsley sprigs,
   to garnish

2 Brush both sides of the fish with the herb butter before placing them in a hinged basket.

3 Barbecue the fish for 5 minutes on one side, then turn over and cook the other side, basting with the remaining herb butter.

4 Just before serving, sprinkle over the lemon juice. Garnish the trout with Swiss chard leaves and flat leaf parsley sprigs.

1 Stir together the butter, dill and flat leaf parsley and season to taste with salt and pepper.

VARIATION: You might like to try substituting fresh coriander for the dill and flat leaf parsley used here.

COOK'S TIP: You can also barbecue whole rainbow trout. Brush with the herb butter as for the fillets, but before placing the fish in a hinged basket, brush the heads and tails with a little water and dip in granular salt to prevent them from burning.

Sea Bream with Fennel, Mustard & Orange

Sea bream is a revelation to anyone unfamiliar with its creamy rich flavour. It has a firm white flesh that goes well with the rich butter sauce.

Serves 2

INGREDIENTS
2 x 350 g/12 oz sea bream, cleaned
   and scaled
10 ml/2 tsp Dijon mustard
5 ml/1 tsp fennel seeds
30 ml/2 tbsp olive oil
50 g/2 oz watercress
175 g/6 oz mixed lettuce leaves
1 orange, segmented
2 jacket potatoes, to serve

FOR THE SAUCE
30 ml/2 tbsp frozen orange juice concentrate
175 g/6 oz/¾ cup unsalted butter, diced
salt and cayenne pepper

2 Slash the bream four times on either side. Combine the mustard and fennel seeds, then spread over both sides of the fish. Moisten with oil and place in a hinged basket. Barbecue for 12 minutes, turning once.

COOK'S TIP: Potatoes, pricked, brushed with oil and wrapped in foil, can be baked on the barbecue, but take a long time and the skin often chars into hard patches.

An easy alternative is to bake the wrapped potatoes in the oven until nearly done and then finish them off on the barbecue while you are cooking the fish.

Alternatively, cut into four wedges and parboil in lightly salted water for about 5 minutes. Drain and toss in oil and then cook on the barbecue for about 15 minutes, turning frequently.

1 For the sauce, place the orange juice concentrate in a bowl and heat over 2.5 cm/1 in boiling water. Remove from the heat, and gradually whisk in the butter until creamy. Season to taste, cover and set aside.

3 Moisten the watercress and lettuce leaves with the remaining olive oil, arrange the fish on two large plates and put the mixed leaves and orange segments to one side. Spoon the orange butter sauce over the fish and serve with jacket potatoes.

Fish Parcels

Sea bass is good for this recipe, but you could also use small whole trout, or white fish fillets, such as cod or haddock.

Serves 4

INGREDIENTS
4 pieces sea bass fillet or 4 cleaned
    whole small sea bass, about
    450 g/1 lb each
oil, for brushing
2 shallots, thinly sliced
1 garlic clove, chopped
15 ml/1 tbsp capers
6 sun-dried tomatoes, finely chopped
4 black olives, pitted and thinly sliced
grated rind and juice of 1 lemon
5 ml/1 tsp paprika
salt and freshly ground black pepper
crusty bread, to serve
fresh flat leaf parsley sprigs, to garnish

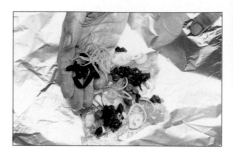

3 Scatter over the shallots, garlic, capers, tomatoes, olives and grated lemon rind. Sprinkle with the lemon juice and paprika.

1 Cut four large squares of double-thickness foil, large enough to enclose the fish. Brush with a little oil.

4 Fold the foil over to enclose the fish loosely, sealing the edges firmly so none of the juices can escape. Place on a moderately hot barbecue and cook for 8–10 minutes. Then open up the tops of the parcels and serve with crusty bread, garnished with parsley.

2 Place a piece of fish in the centre of each piece of foil and season well with salt and pepper.

COOK'S TIP: To bake in the oven: place on a baking sheet and cook at 200°C/400°F/Gas 6 for 20 minutes.

Red Mullet with Lavender

Cook up a barbecue with a difference by adding lavender to fresh mullet for a delicious aromatic flavour.

Serves 4

INGREDIENTS
4 red mullet, cleaned and scaled
45 ml/3 tbsp fresh lavender flowers or
    15 ml/1 tbsp dried lavender flowers,
    roughly chopped
juice and coarsely grated rind of 1 lemon
4 spring onions, roughly chopped
60 ml/4 tbsp olive oil
salt and freshly ground black pepper

COOK'S TIP: Sprinkle some
lavender flowers on the hot coals
while cooking the fish.

1 Place the mullet in a large shallow dish. Mix together the lavender flowers, lemon juice and rind, spring onions and olive oil and season to taste with salt and pepper. Pour over the fish, cover and set aside to marinate for at least 3 hours.

2 Drain off the marinade and discard the lemon rind. Place the mullet in a hinged basket and cook on a very hot barbecue for 5–7 minutes on each side, brushing with the marinade from time to time.

Italian Prawn Skewers

Prawns cook in minutes, but are among the most delicious of tempting treats from the barbecue.

Serves 4

INGREDIENTS
900 g/2 lb raw tiger prawns, peeled
60 ml/4 tbsp olive oil
45 ml/3 tbsp vegetable oil
75 g/3 oz/1¼ cups very fine
    dry breadcrumbs
1 garlic clove, crushed
15 ml/1 tbsp chopped fresh parsley
salt and freshly ground
    black pepper
lemon wedges, to serve

1 Slit the prawns down their backs and remove the dark vein. Rinse in cold water and pat dry.

2 Put the olive oil and vegetable oil in a large bowl and add the prawns, mixing them to coat evenly. Add the breadcrumbs, garlic and parsley and season with salt and pepper. Toss the prawns thoroughly, to give them an even coating of breadcrumbs. Cover and leave to marinate for 1 hour.

3 Thread the prawns on to four metal or wooden skewers, curling them up as you do so, so that the tail is skewered in the middle. Place the skewers on the barbecue and cook for about 2 minutes on each side, until the breadcrumbs are golden. Serve with lemon wedges.

Barbecued Scallops with Lime Butter

Fresh scallops are quick to cook and ideal for barbecues. This recipe combines them simply with lime and fennel.

Serves 4

INGREDIENTS
1 head fennel
2 limes
12 large scallops, cleaned
1 egg yolk
90 ml/6 tbsp melted butter
oil, for brushing
salt and freshly ground black pepper

1 Trim any feathery leaves from the fennel and reserve them. Slice the rest lengthways into thin wedges.

2 Cut one lime into wedges. Finely grate the rind and squeeze the juice of the other lime and toss half the juice and rind with the scallops. Season well.

COOK'S TIP: Thread small scallops on to flat skewers, to make them easier to turn.

3 Place the egg yolk and remaining lime rind and juice in a bowl and whisk hard until pale and smooth.

4 Gradually whisk in the melted butter and continue whisking until thick and smooth. Finely chop the reserved fennel leaves and stir them in, with seasoning to taste.

5 Brush the fennel wedges with oil and cook them on a hot barbecue for 3–4 minutes, turning once.

6 Add the scallops and cook for a further 3–4 minutes, turning once, until just cooked but still soft. Transfer to a warm plate and serve immediately with the lime and fennel butter and the lime wedges.

Barbecued Jerk Chicken

Jerk refers to the blend of herb and spice seasoning rubbed into meat, before it is roasted over charcoal.

Serves 4

INGREDIENTS
8 chicken pieces
vegetable oil, for brushing
salad leaves, to serve

FOR THE MARINADE
5 ml/1 tsp ground allspice
5 ml/1 tsp ground cinnamon
5 ml/1 tsp dried thyme
1.5 ml/¼ tsp freshly grated nutmeg
10 ml/2 tsp demerara sugar
2 garlic cloves, crushed
15 ml/1 tbsp finely chopped onion
15 ml/1 tbsp chopped spring onion
15 ml/1 tbsp wine vinegar
30 ml/2 tbsp vegetable oil
15 ml/1 tbsp lime juice
1 hot chilli pepper, chopped
salt and freshly ground black pepper

2 Place the chicken pieces in a dish and make several lengthways slits in the flesh. Rub the marinade all over the chicken and into the slits. Cover with clear film and marinate overnight in the fridge.

3 When you are ready to cook the chicken shake off any excess marinade. Brush the chicken with oil and place on the barbecue grill. Cook for about 30 minutes, turning often to ensure even browning. Serve the chicken hot with salad leaves.

COOK'S TIP: If you prefer a less spicy marinade, remove and discard the fiery seeds from the chilli pepper before mixing with the rest of the marinade ingredients.

1 Combine all the marinade ingredients in a small bowl. Using a fork, mash them together well to form a thick paste.

Barbecued Chicken with Pica de Gallo Salsa

This dish originates from Mexico. Its hot fruity flavours form the essence of Tex-Mex cooking.

Serves 4

INGREDIENTS
4 chicken breasts
pinch of celery salt and cayenne
    pepper combined
30 ml/2 tbsp vegetable oil
fresh coriander sprigs, to garnish
corn chips, to serve

FOR THE SALSA
275 g/10 oz watermelon
175 g/6 oz canteloupe melon
1 small red onion
1–2 green chillies
30 ml/2 tbsp lime juice
60 ml/4 tbsp chopped
    fresh coriander
pinch of salt

1 First, make the salsa. Remove the rind and as many seeds as you can from the melons. Finely dice the flesh and put it into a bowl.

2 Finely chop the onion, split the chillies (discarding the seeds which contain most of the heat) and chop. Take care not to touch sensitive skin areas when handling cut chillies. Mix with the melon.

3 Add the lime juice and chopped coriander, and season with a pinch of salt. Turn the salsa into a small bowl and set aside in the fridge.

4 Slash the chicken breasts deeply to speed up the cooking time. Season the chicken with celery salt and cayenne, and brush with oil. Place on the barbecue and cook for about 15 minutes, turning frequently.

5 Arrange the chicken on a plate, garnish with coriander and serve with the salsa and a handful of corn chips.

Turkey Breasts with Tomato-corn Relish

Tasty, economical and quick, turkey breasts are ideal for the barbecue.

Serves 4

INGREDIENTS
4 skinless boneless turkey breast halves,
    about 175 g/6 oz each
30 ml/2 tbsp fresh lemon juice
30 ml/2 tbsp olive oil
2.5 ml/½ tsp ground cumin
2.5 ml/½ tsp dried oregano
5 ml/1 tsp coarse black pepper
salt
mixed salad leaves, to serve

FOR THE RELISH
1 fresh hot green chilli
450 g/1 lb tomatoes, seeded and chopped
250 g/9 oz/1½ cups corn kernels, freshly
    cooked or thawed frozen
3 spring onions, chopped
15 ml/1 tbsp chopped fresh parsley
30 ml/2 tbsp chopped fresh coriander
30 ml/2 tbsp fresh lemon juice
45 ml/3 tbsp olive oil
5 ml/1 tsp salt

1 With a meat mallet, pound the turkey breasts between two sheets of greaseproof paper until thin.

COOK'S TIP: Use the cooked turkey, thinly sliced and combined with the relish, as a filling for warmed flour tortillas.

2 In a shallow dish, combine the lemon juice, oil, cumin, oregano and pepper. Add the turkey and turn to coat. Cover and set aside for 2 hours, or refrigerate overnight.

3 For the relish, grill the chilli or roast over a gas flame, holding it with tongs, until charred on all sides. When cooled, carefully rub off the skin. For a less hot flavour, discard the seeds. Chop the chilli finely and place in a bowl.

4 Add to the chilli the remaining relish ingredients and toss well to blend. Set aside.

5 Remove the turkey from the marinade. Season lightly on both sides with salt to taste.

6 Put the turkey breasts on the barbecue and cook for 2–3 minutes, until browned. Turn and cook on the other side for 3–4 minutes, until it is cooked through. Serve the turkey immediately, accompanied by the tomato relish and salad leaves.

Chicken Kebabs with Tangy Citrus Marinade

Serve on a bed of lettuce leaves and garnish with fresh mint and orange and lemon slices.

Serves 4

INGREDIENTS
4 boneless, skinless chicken breasts
fresh mint sprigs, and orange, lemon or
    lime slices, to garnish (optional)

FOR THE MARINADE
finely grated rind and juice of ½ orange
finely grated rind and juice of ½ small lemon
    or lime
30 ml/2 tbsp olive oil
30 ml/2 tbsp clear honey
30 ml/2 tbsp chopped fresh mint
1.5 ml/¼ tsp ground cumin
salt and freshly ground black pepper

1 With a sharp knife, cut the chicken into cubes of about 2.5 cm/1 in.

2 Mix all the marinade ingredients together, add the chicken cubes and toss to coat well. Set to marinate for at least 2 hours.

3 Thread the chicken pieces on to skewers and barbecue for 15 minutes over low coals on the coolest part of the rack (or raise an adjustable rack). Baste with the marinade and turn frequently. Serve the kebabs garnished with extra mint and citrus slices if desired.

Char-grilled Sausages with Prunes & Bacon

Sausages are a constant barbecue favourite and this is one way to ring the changes. Serve with crusty bread.

Serves 4

INGREDIENTS
8 large, meaty sausages, such as Toulouse or
    good-quality pork sausages
30 ml/2 tbsp Dijon mustard
24 ready-to-eat prunes
8 smoked streaky bacon rashers

1 With a sharp knife, cut a long slit through one side of each sausage, cutting them about three-quarters of the way through.

2 Spread the cut surface with mustard and then place three prunes in each sausage, pressing them in firmly.

3 Gently stretch the bacon rashers out thinly with the back of a round-bladed knife. Wrap round the sausages, securing with cocktail sticks.

4 Cook the sausages over a hot barbecue for 15–18 minutes, turning occasionally, until evenly browned and thoroughly cooked.

Lamb Kebabs

Kebabs are always a good choice for the barbecue as they are easy to handle and look very colourful and appetizing.

Serves 6

INGREDIENTS
675 g/1½ lb lean lamb, cut into
    4 cm/1½ in cubes
12 shallots or button onions
2 green peppers, seeded and cut
    into 12 pieces
12 small tomatoes
12 small mushrooms
rosemary sprigs, to garnish
lemon slices, to garnish
cooked rice and crusty bread, to serve

FOR THE MARINADE
juice of 1 lemon
120 ml/4 fl oz/½ cup red wine
1 onion, finely chopped
60 ml/4 tbsp olive oil
2.5 ml/½ tsp each dried sage and rosemary
salt and freshly ground black pepper

1 For the marinade, combine the lemon juice, red wine, onion, olive oil, herbs and seasoning in a bowl.

2 Stir the cubes of lamb into the marinade. Cover and refrigerate for 2–12 hours, stirring occasionally.

VARIATION: To vary this recipe sprinkle over 30 ml/2 tbsp chopped fresh parsley and finely chopped onion, to garnish.

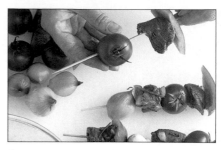

3 Remove the lamb from the marinade and thread on to six skewers, alternating with the shallots or onions, peppers, tomatoes and mushrooms.

4 Cook the kebabs over the hot coals of a barbecue for 10–15 minutes, turning them once. Use the leftover marinade to brush over the kebabs during cooking to prevent the meat from drying out.

5 To serve the kebabs place them on a bed of freshly cooked rice. Garnish with fresh rosemary and lemon slices and accompany with crusty bread.

Racks of Lamb with Lavender & Balsamic Vinegar

Lavender is an unusual flavour to use with meat, but its heady, summery scent really works well with grilled lamb.

Serves 4

INGREDIENTS
4 racks of lamb, with 3–4 cutlets each
1 shallot, finely chopped
45 ml/3 tbsp chopped fresh lavender
15 ml/1 tbsp balsamic vinegar
30 ml/2 tbsp olive oil
15 ml/1 tbsp lemon juice
salt and freshly ground
  black pepper
handful of lavender sprigs

2 Sprinkle the lavender over the lamb. Beat together the vinegar, oil and lemon juice and pour them over the lamb, reserving some of the marinade for basting. Season well with salt and freshly ground pepper and then turn to coat evenly.

1 Place the racks of lamb in a large bowl or wide dish and sprinkle over the chopped shallot.

VARIATION: Individual lamb cutlets can also be cooked in this way; allow 10–15 minutes, turning occasionally. You can substitute rosemary or thyme for the lavender, if preferred.

3 Scatter a few lavender sprigs on the coals of a medium-hot barbecue. Cook the lamb for 15–20 minutes, turning once and basting with any remaining marinade, until golden brown and still slightly pink in the centre.

Minced Lamb & Beef Kebabs

In the Middle East, these kebabs are known as *Kabab Kobideh* and are often served with rice stirred with raw egg yolk and melted butter.

Serves 6–8

INGREDIENTS
450 g/1 lb lean lamb
450 g/1 lb lean beef
1 large onion, grated
2 garlic cloves, crushed
15 ml/1 tbsp sumac (optional)
2–3 saffron strands, soaked in 15 ml/1 tbsp
    boiling water
10 ml/2 tsp bicarbonate of soda
6–8 tomatoes, halved
15 ml/1 tbsp melted butter
salt and freshly ground black pepper
cooked rice, to serve

1 Mince the lamb and beef two or three times until very fine. Place in a large bowl and add the grated onion, garlic, sumac, if using, soaked saffron, bicarbonate of soda and salt and pepper.

2 Knead by hand until the mixture is very glutinous. It helps to have a bowl of water nearby in which to dip your fingers to stop the meat sticking.

3 Take a small handful of meat and roll it into a ball. If the ball seems crumbly, knead the mixture in the bowl for a few more minutes.

4 Shape the ball around a flat skewer, moulding it around. Repeat with three or four more balls on each skewer, pressing them tightly to prevent the meat from falling off.

5 Carefully thread all of the tomato halves on to two or three separate metal or soaked wooden skewers.

6 When the coals are ready, grill the meat and tomato kebabs for about 10 minutes, basting them with the butter and turning occasionally. Serve on a bed of rice.

COOK'S TIP: Sumac is a favourite Lebanese spice with a slightly sour but fruity flavour. It is available from most Middle Eastern food shops, but it is not essential in this recipe.

Beef & Mushroom Burgers

Nothing compares with the succulence and flavour of home-made burgers. Here they are flavoured with onions, mushrooms and herbs.

Serves 4

INGREDIENTS
1 small onion, chopped
150 g/5 oz/2 cups small
  cup mushrooms
450 g/1 lb lean minced beef
50 g/2 oz/1 cup fresh
  wholemeal breadcrumbs
5 ml/1 tsp dried mixed herbs
15 ml/1 tbsp tomato purée
flour, for shaping
salt and freshly ground
  black pepper
salad and burger buns or
  pitta bread, to serve

1 Place the onion and mushrooms in a food processor and process until finely chopped. Add the beef, breadcrumbs, herbs, tomato purée and seasonings. Process for a few seconds, until the mixture binds together but still has some texture.

2 Divide the meat mixture into 8–12 pieces, then press into burger shapes using lightly floured hands.

3 Cook the burgers on a medium barbecue for 12–15 minutes, turning once, until evenly cooked. Serve with salad, in burger buns or pitta bread.

Sizzling Asian Steak

This is a Malaysian method of sizzling meat on a hot barbecue.

Serves 4–6

INGREDIENTS
4 x 200 g/7 oz rump steaks
1 garlic clove, crushed
2.5 cm/1 in piece of fresh root ginger,
   finely chopped
10 ml/2 tsp black peppercorns
15 ml/1 tbsp sugar
30 ml/2 tbsp tamarind sauce
45 ml/3 tbsp dark soy sauce
15 ml/1 tbsp oyster sauce
vegetable oil, for brushing
carrots and spring onions, shredded, to garnish

FOR THE DIPPING SAUCE
75 ml/5 tbsp/⅓ cup beef stock
30 ml/2 tbsp tomato ketchup
5 ml/1 tsp chilli sauce
juice of 1 lime

1 Place the steaks in a shallow dish. Pound together the garlic, ginger, peppercorns, sugar, tamarind sauce, soy sauce and oyster sauce in a mortar with a pestle. Spoon the marinade over the steaks, turning to coat thoroughly. Set aside to marinate for up to 8 hours.

2 Scrape the marinade from the meat and place in a pan. Add the stock, tomato ketchup, chilli sauce and lime juice and simmer briefly. Keep warm on the side of the barbecue.

3 Brush the steaks with oil and cook on the barbecue for 2 minutes on each side, or according to taste. Garnish with the shredded carrots and spring onions. Serve the steaks with the dipping sauce.

Grilled Mediterranean Vegetables with Marbled Pesto

This is a meal on its own, or delicious served as an accompaniment. Look out for baby vegetables, such as baby aubergines and peppers.

Serves 4

INGREDIENTS
2 small aubergines
2 large courgettes
1 red pepper
1 yellow pepper
1 fennel bulb
1 red onion
olive oil, for brushing

FOR THE SAUCE
150 ml/¼ pint/⅔ cup Greek-style yogurt
45 ml/3 tbsp pesto
salt and freshly ground
    black pepper

1 Cut the aubergines into 1 cm/½ in thick slices. Sprinkle with salt and leave to drain in a colander for about 30 minutes. Rinse and dry well with a dish towel or kitchen paper.

2 Cut the courgettes in half lengthways. Cut the peppers in half, remove the seeds but leave the stalk on. Slice the fennel bulb and the onion into fairly thick wedges.

3 Stir the yogurt and pesto lightly together, to make a marbled sauce. Spoon into a serving bowl.

4 Arrange the vegetables on the hot barbecue, brush with oil and sprinkle with salt and pepper.

5 Cook the vegetables until golden brown and tender, turning them occasionally. The aubergines and peppers will take 6–8 minutes to cook, the courgettes, onion and fennel 4–5 minutes. Serve with the marbled pesto sauce.

Herb Polenta with Grilled Tomatoes

Golden polenta with fresh summer herbs and sweet grilled tomatoes is the perfect vegetarian barbecue.

Serves 4

INGREDIENTS
750 ml/1¼ pints/3 cups stock or water
5 ml/1 tsp salt
175 g/6 oz/1 cup polenta
25 g/1 oz/2 tbsp butter
75 ml/5 tbsp mixed chopped fresh parsley,
    chives and basil, plus extra, to garnish
olive oil, for brushing
4 large plum or beefsteak tomatoes, halved
salt and freshly ground black pepper

1 Prepare the polenta in advance. Place the stock or water in a pan with the salt, bring to the boil, then reduce the heat and stir in the polenta. Stir constantly over a moderate heat for 5 minutes, until the polenta begins to thicken and come away from the sides of the pan.

2 Remove from the heat and stir in the butter, herbs and black pepper.

3 Tip the mixture into a wide, greased tin or dish and spread it out evenly. Leave until it is completely cool and set.

4 Turn out the polenta and cut it into squares or stamp out rounds with a large biscuit cutter. Brush the slices with olive oil.

COOK'S TIP: Any mixture of fresh herbs can be used, or try using just basil or chives alone, for a really distinctive flavour.

5 Brush the tomatoes with oil and sprinkle with salt and pepper. Cook the tomatoes and polenta on a medium-hot barbecue for 5 minutes, turning once. Serve garnished with fresh herbs.

Tofu Satay

Barbecue cubes of smoked tofu (soya beancurd) until golden and crispy, then serve with a Thai-style peanut sauce.

Serves 4–6

INGREDIENTS
2 x 200 g/7 oz packs smoked tofu
  (soya beancurd)
45 ml/3 tbsp light soy sauce
10 ml/2 tsp sesame oil
1 garlic clove, crushed
1 yellow and 1 red pepper, seeded
8–12 fresh bay leaves
sunflower oil, for grilling

FOR THE DIPPING SAUCE
2 spring onions, finely chopped
2 garlic cloves, crushed
pinch of chilli powder or a few drops of
  hot chilli sauce
5 ml/1 tsp sugar
15 ml/1 tbsp white vinegar
30 ml/2 tbsp light soy sauce
45 ml/3 tbsp crunchy peanut butter

1 Cut the tofu into bite-size cubes and mix with the soy sauce, sesame oil and garlic. Cover and marinate for 20 minutes.

2 Beat the sauce ingredients together until well blended. Avoid using a food processor for this, as the texture should be slightly chunky.

3 Cut the peppers into squares. Drain the tofu and thread the cubes on to 8–12 wooden satay sticks with the pepper squares and bay leaves. Larger leaves may need to be halved.

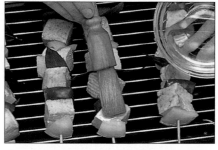

4 Brush the satays with oil. Cook on the barbecue, turning the sticks occasionally, until the ingredients are browned and crisp. Serve hot with the dipping sauce.

Aubergine, Tomato & Feta Rolls

Barbecued aubergines wrapped around tangy feta cheese, flavoured with basil and sun-dried tomatoes, make a wonderfully summery combination.

Serves 4

INGREDIENTS
2 large aubergines
olive oil
10–12 sun-dried tomatoes
   in oil, drained
handful of large, fresh
   basil leaves
150 g/5 oz feta cheese
salt and freshly ground
   black pepper
ciabatta bread, to serve

2 Rinse the aubergines in cold water and dry well. Brush with oil on both sides and grill on a hot barbecue for 2–3 minutes, turning once, until golden brown and softened.

1 Slice the aubergines lengthways into 5 mm/¼ in thick slices. Sprinkle with salt and layer in a colander. Leave to drain for about 30 minutes.

VARIATION: Vegans could use tofu (soya beancurd) in place of the feta. Sprinkle with soy sauce before wrapping.

3 Arrange the sun-dried tomatoes over one end of each aubergine slice and top with the basil leaves. Cut the feta cheese into short sticks and place on top. Season with salt and freshly ground black pepper.

4 Carefully roll the aubergine slices around to enclose the filling. Cook the rolls on the barbecue for a further 2–3 minutes, until they are hot. Serve with ciabatta bread.

Barbecued Goat's Cheese Pizza

Pizzas cooked on the barbecue have a beautifully crisp and golden base, which contrasts deliciously with the melt-in-the-mouth topping.

Serves 4

INGREDIENTS
150 g/5 oz packet pizza-base mix
olive oil, for brushing
150 ml/¼ pint/⅔ cup passata
30 ml/2 tbsp red pesto sauce
1 small red onion, thinly sliced
8 cherry tomatoes, halved
115 g/4 oz firm goat's cheese, thinly sliced
handful chopped fresh basil leaves
salt and freshly ground black pepper

1 Make up the pizza dough, according to the packet instructions. Roll it out to a round of about 25 cm/10 in diameter.

2 Brush the dough with oil and place, oiled side down, on a medium–hot barbecue. Cook for about 6–8 minutes, until firm and golden underneath.

3 Brush the top of the dough with oil and turn the dough over, to cook the other side for 6 minutes.

COOK'S TIP: If the pizza starts to brown too much underneath, raise the grill rack away from the fire, or slip a piece of foil under the pizza, to slow down the cooking.

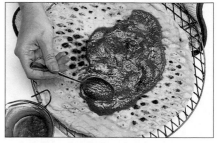

4 Mix together the passata and pesto sauce and quickly spread over the cooked side of the pizza, to within about 1 cm/½ in of the edge.

5 Arrange the sliced onion, halved tomatoes and goat's cheese slices on top and sprinkle with salt and freshly ground black pepper.

6 Cook the pizza on the barbecue for a further 8–10 minutes, or until the dough has turned golden brown and crisp. Sprinkle with chopped basil leaves and serve.

Spiced Pear & Blueberry Parcels

This combination makes a delicious dessert for a special-occasion barbecue on a summer's evening.

Serves 4

INGREDIENTS
4 firm, ripe pears
30 ml/2 tbsp lemon juice
15 ml/1 tbsp melted butter
150 g/5 oz/1¼ cups blueberries
60 ml/4 tbsp light
    muscovado sugar
freshly ground black pepper

2 Brush the pears thoroughly with lemon juice, to prevent them from turning unattractively brown.

3 Cut four squares of double-thickness foil, each large enough to wrap two pear halves, and brush them with melted butter.

1 Peel the pears thinly. Cut them in half lengthways. Scoop out the core from each half, with a teaspoon and a sharp knife.

COOK'S TIP: If you wish to assemble the dessert in advance, place a layer of greaseproof paper inside the parcel, because the acid in the lemon juice may react with the foil and taint the flavour.

4 Place two pear halves on each piece of foil, with the cut sides upwards. Gather the foil up around the pears, to hold them level.

5 Mix the blueberries and sugar together and spoon them on top of the pears.

6 Sprinkle with black pepper. Wrap the foil over and cook on a fairly hot barbecue for 20–25 minutes.

Chargrilled Apples on Cinnamon Toasts

This simple, scrumptious dessert is best made with an enriched bread, such as brioche, but any light, sweet bread will do.

Serves 4

INGREDIENTS
4 sweet eating apples
juice of ½ lemon
4 individual brioches or muffins
60 ml/4 tbsp melted butter
30 ml/2 tbsp golden caster sugar
5 ml/1 tsp ground cinnamon
cream or Greek-style yogurt,
   to serve

1 Core the apples and then cut them horizontally in three to four thick slices. Sprinkle with lemon juice.

2 Cut the brioches or muffins into thick slices. Brush with melted butter on both sides.

3 Mix together the caster sugar and the ground cinnamon in a small bowl until well combined.

4 Place the apple and brioche slices on the hot barbecue and cook them for 3–4 minutes, turning once, until they are beginning to turn golden brown.

5 Sprinkle half the cinnamon sugar over the apple slices and toasts and cook for a further minute, until they are a rich golden brown.

6 To serve, arrange the apple slices over the toasts and sprinkle them with the remaining cinnamon sugar. Serve hot, with cream or yogurt.

Baked Bananas with Spicy Vanilla Butter

Baked bananas are a must for the barbecue – they're so easy because they bake in their own skins and need no preparation at all.

Serves 4

INGREDIENTS
4 bananas
6 green cardamom pods
1 vanilla pod
finely grated rind of 1 small orange
30 ml/2 tbsp brandy or orange juice
60 ml/4 tbsp light muscovado sugar
45 ml/3 tbsp butter
crème fraîche or Greek-style yogurt,
   to serve (optional)

2 Meanwhile, split the cardamom pods and remove the seeds. Crush lightly using a pestle and mortar.

3 Split the vanilla pod lengthways and scrape out the tiny seeds. Mix with the cardamom seeds, orange rind, brandy or orange juice, sugar and butter, into a thick paste.

1 Place the bananas, in their skins, on the hot barbecue and leave for 6–8 minutes, turning occasionally, until becoming brownish-black.

VARIATION: The flavoured butter is not essential, but adds extra richness to the bananas. Children may prefer melted chocolate, jam or honey on their bananas.

4 Slit the skin of each banana, open out slightly and spoon in a little of the paste. Serve with a spoonful of crème fraîche or Greek-style yogurt, if using.

Oranges in Maple & Cointreau Syrup

This is one of the most delicious ways to eat an orange, and a luxurious way to round off a barbecue party.

Serves 4

INGREDIENTS
20 ml/4 tsp butter, plus extra, melted,
    for brushing
4 medium-size oranges
30 ml/2 tbsp maple syrup
30 ml/2 tbsp Cointreau or Grand
    Marnier liqueur
crème fraîche or fromage frais,
    to serve

1 Cut four double-thickness squares of foil, large enough to wrap the oranges. Brush the centre of each with melted butter.

2 Remove some shreds of orange rind, to decorate. Blanch them, dry them and set them aside. Peel the oranges, removing all the white pith and peel and catching any juice that escapes in a bowl.

3 Slice the oranges crossways into several thick slices. Reassemble them and place each on a square of foil.

4 Tuck the foil up around the oranges, to keep them in shape, leaving the foil open at the top.

5 Mix together the reserved orange juice, maple syrup and liqueur and spoon the mixture over the oranges.

VARIATION: For an alcohol-free version of this dish, omit the liqueur.

6 Add a dab of butter to each parcel and fold over the foil to seal in the juices. Place the parcels on a hot barbecue for 10–12 minutes, until hot. Serve with crème fraîche or fromage frais, topped with the prepared shreds of orange rind.

First published in 1999 by Hermes House

© Anness Publishing Limited 1999

Hermes House is an imprint of
Anness Publishing Limited
Hermes House
88-89 Blackfriars Road
London SE1 8HA

A CIP catalogue record for this book is available from the British Library

Publisher: Joanna Lorenz
Editor: Valerie Ferguson
Series Designer: Bobbie Colgate Stone
Designer: Andrew Heath
Editorial Reader: Penelope Goodare
Production Controller: Joanna King

Recipes Contributed by: Catherine Atkinson, Angela Boggiano, Carla Capalbo, Lesley Chamberlain, Trisha Davies,
Roz Denny, Nicola Diggins, Joanna Farrow, Christine France, Silvano Franco, Rosamund Grant, Deh-Ta Hsiung,
Soheila Kimberley, Sue Maggs, Liz Trigg, Laura Washburn, Steven Wheeler, Jenni Wright.

Photography: Karl Adamson, Edward Allwright, James Duncan, Ian Garlick, Michelle Garrett,
Amanda Heywood, Janine Hosegood, David Jordan, Don Last, William Lingwood, Patrick McLeavey, Michael Michaels.

1 3 5 7 9 10 8 6 4 2

Notes:
For all recipes, quantities are given in both metric and imperial measures and,
where appropriate, measures are also given in standard cups and spoons.
Follow one set, but not a mixture, because they are
not interchangeable.

Standard spoon and cup measures are level.

1 tsp = 5 ml   1 tbsp = 15 ml

1 cup = 250 ml/8 fl oz

Australian standard tablespoons are 20 ml.
Australian readers should use 3 tsp in place of 1 tbsp for measuring small quantities of gelatine,
cornflour, salt, etc.

Medium eggs are used unless otherwise stated.

Printed and bound in Singapore